For more laughs get these other LOL books now:

ISBN: 978-1642502329

Squeaky Clean Super Funny Jokes for Kidz

ISBN: 978-1642502343

Squeaky Clean Super Funny Knock Knock Jokes for Kidz

ISBN: 978-1642502381

Squeaky Clean Super Funny School Jokes for Kidz

SQUEAKY CLEAN SUPER FUNNY

RIDDLES!

for kidz

LOL!

Written and illustrated by Craig Yoe

mango

CORAL GABLES

For permission requests, please contact the publisher at:

Mango Publishing Group

2850 S Douglas Road, 2nd Floor

Coral Gables, FL 33134 USA

info@mango.bz

For special orders, quantity sales, course adoptions and corporate sales, please email the publisher at sales@mango.bz. For trade and wholesale sales, please contact Ingram Publisher Services at customer.service@ingramcontent.com or +1.800.509.4887.

Squeaky Clean Super Funny Riddles for Kidz

Library of Congress Cataloging-in-Publication number: Has been requested

ISBN: (print) 978-1-64250-238-1, (ebook) 978-1-64250-239-8

BISAC category code JUVENILE NONFICTION, Humor / Jokes & Riddles

Printed in the United States of America

CONTENTS

Chapter 1

A Hoot and a Half!

What's the best day to adopt a rescue kitten?

CAT-urday!

Leah: What did the mamma train say to the baby train?

Mia: "CHEW-CHEW your food!"

What does a robin serve at parties?

BIRD-day cake!

What fruit is yellow and blue?

A sad banana!

Q: What can't you eat for breakfast?
A: Lunch and dinner! LOL!

Bev: What did the sesame seed say to the hamburger bun?

Kev: "I'm on a ROLL!"

What does a motorcycle rider order at a hotel?
V-ROOM service! :)

What kind of vehicle does a golfer drive?

A FORE-by-FORE! ROTFL!

Where do rabbits go after they get married?

On a BUNNY-moon!

What did the third base coach tell the baseball player?

"There's no place like HOME!" HA HA HA!

Bella: What do you call a pair of chickens?

Stella: Two O'CLUCK!

Eli: How do you get a truck without an engine to run?

Levi: Put a hill under it!

What do you get when you combine a computer with a cashew?

The inter-NUT! CHORTLE!

What does the class clown wear to school?

A TEE-HEE shirt!

What veggie does a phone like to eat?

CELL-ery!

What's a lion's favorite fruit?

GRRR-apes!

Chapter 2

Crack-Ups!

What is a giraffe's favorite fruit?

NECK-tarines! HA HA HA!

What game does a slice of pizza like to play?

Tic-tac-DOUGH! LOL!

Where do plants take naps?

In FLOWER BEDS!

What's an astronaut's favorite day of the week?

MOON-day!

Zoe: When is a bed bad?

Joey: When it encourages you to lie!

Where do chickens like to eat?

At the ROOSTER-ant! HA HA HA!

Alex: What is at the end of the road?

Alexis: The letter D!

What kind of computer does a frog use?
A LEAP-top! GUFFAW!

What do you have to remember to do to the closet doors?

CLOTHES them!

Why did the bee get a prize?

For good BEE-havior! LOL!

Jim: Why did the firefly feel sick?

Kim: It had GLOWING pains!

Q: What word is always pronounced wrong?

A: Wrong! LOL!

> **What word is always pronounced right?**
> Com'on, you can guess this one, right?!

What bird can lift the most weight?

A crane!

What kind of berry has a sore throat?

A RASPY-berry! :)

What is the correct way to get down from a horse?

You can't get down from a horse. You get DOWN from a DUCK!

What should a teacher know before teaching his class?

More than the class! LOL!

> **Jaxon:** What does a queen do in a fire?
> **Jessica:** Stop, drop, and RULE!

Why isn't a nose twelve inches long?

Because then it would be a FOOT! LOL!

Why was the rattlesnake so popular?

It had a great POISON-ality!

What do you call a hog's autobiography?

A PIG-tale!

Colton: What's a reporter's favorite food?

Cameron: Ice cream. They love to get a scoop! ROTFL!

Why does the Statue of Liberty stand in New York Harbor?

Because she can't sit down!

What kind of bugs are found in an apartment building?

Occup-ANTS!

Moe: What do you call a cow with four short legs?

Joe: A COW-ch!

Q: What did the bee say to the rose?

A: "You're my best bud!"

What's the best way to keep a popsicle from melting?

Eat it! GUFFAW!

How many feet are in a yard?

That depends on how many people are standing in it!

Amelia: What do you do before getting off your bicycle?

Zoe: Get on it!

What's a cow's favorite day of the week?
MOOS-day!

What day are you most likely to get a tummy ache?

MOAN-day!

What did the man do when he broke his foot?
He called the TOE truck! HA HA HA!

Moe: Why did the cow cross the road?

Joe: She wanted to go to the MOO-vies!

What do you call a rabbit who thinks positive?
A HOP-timist!

Chapter 3

Funny as a Barrel of Monkeys!

What's a police officer's favorite food?

Corn on the COP! :)

Why do bears have fur and live in a cave?

So you can tell them apart from grapes! CHORTLE!

Larry: Where does January come after February?

Mary: In the dictionary!

Why kind of cow likes to play baseball?

A base-BULL!

What do baseball players put in front of their houses?

A welcome MITT! LOL!

Why don't cows vacation on cruise ships?

They get MOO-tion sickness!

What's a dog's favorite snack?

PUP-corn!

Q: What did the mosquito say to its kid at bedtime?
A: "Good BITE!"

What do you say to your teacher the last day of school?

"Keep in TEACH!"

When you are at the top of a ladder, what continent do you see?

You're up! (Europe!)

Griff: What tool do you use to build a playground?
Biff: A SEE-saw! CHORTLE!

What kind of school did the bee go to?

BUZZ-ness school!

This: What did the dad snake do when he put his kid to bed?

That: Gave her a good-night HISS!

Which is the tallest building in town?

The library. It has the most stories!

Ned: What is the opposite of a hair dryer?

Jed: A feet wetter! HA HA HA!

Why did the letter A go to the school nurse?

It was in pain!

Why did the bathtub take a nap?
It felt totally drained!

Q: What's a snake's favorite school subject?

A: HISS-tory!

Jack: Why is the nose in the middle of the face?

Zack: Because that's the SCENT-er! :)

How does a lumberjack play video games?
By LOGGING onto the computer!

What do you call a cat with straight As on their report card?

PURR-fect! LOL!

Why did the pony get grounded?
It was horsing around!

What do you call the landmark that ate too may crepes?

The I-FULL Tower!

What roof is always wet?

The roof of your mouth! HEE-HEE!

What animal is black, white, and purple?

A zebra eating a grape!

What do you call the landmark with sausage and cheese?

The Leaning Tower of PIZZA! LOL!

Where does a caped crusader buy their food?
At the SUPER-market!

Why does a red dog scratch its left ear?

Because it itches!

> **Griffin:** What do you call the landmark
> that takes it easy?
>
> **Grace:** Mount Rush-LESS!

Why did the chicken cross the playground?

To get to the other SLIDE! ROTFL!

What's the coldest letter in the alphabet?

Ice-T!

What game does a bird like to play?

Hide-and-BEAK!

How do say "spaghetti" in Italian!?

"Spaghetti in Italian!" HA HA HA!

What did the groceries say when they were tired?
"We're ready to hit the sack!"

What's a piece of bread's favorite amusement park ride?

A roller TOASTER! GUFFAW!

What is the smartest insect?

A spelling bee!

What kind of boat does a college student travel on?

A SCHOLAR-ship!

What does a mountain use to play baseball?
A sum-MITT! LOL!

What did the runner want on her hamburger?
CATCH-up!

Why was the animal shelter so busy?

Because it was raining cats and dogs!

What's a dog's favorite melon?

A PANT-PANT-aloupe!

What bird is the bravest?

The BOLD eagle!

Laugh Yourself Silly!

When did the chicken cross the road?

At EGGS-actly the right time!

What doesn't a commuter like on bread?

TRAFFIC jam! LOL!

What kind of vehicle does a tree drive?
A FIR-by-FIR!

What kind of soup do dogs like?

Chicken POODLE! :)

What looks like half an apple pie?

The other half!

Sue: How does a cartoonist get to work?

Stu: In a car-TOON!

What is a chicken's favorite dessert?

A COOP cake! HEE-HEE!

What did the sailor get on their report card?

High Cs! HA HA HA!

What do nervous carpenters do?

Bite their nails! LOL!

What happened to the brown stone when it was thrown in the Red Sea?

It got wet!

What is a kitten after it's seven months old?

Eight months old!

How can you keep a dog from running into the street?

Put it in a BARKING lot! HA HA HA!

How do you keep a pig from running into the street?

Put it in a PORKING lot!

Who always whistles while he works?

A football referee!

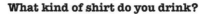

What kind of shirt do you drink?
A TEA shirt!

What is a farm animal's favorite pasta?
Spa-GOAT-ti! GUFFAW!

What did the snake wear to the school prom?

A BOA-tie!

Where did the worm go on vacation?
To the Big Apple!

Where was the snake born?
In the HISS-pital!

What did the target say after the arrow missed him?

"I had an ARROW escape!"

What do you call a stand-up comedian at the beach?

A LAUGH-guard!

When are two heads not better than one?

When you have to pay for hats!

Why did the gorilla wear a catcher's mitt?
He wanted to catch a train!

Punny Jokes!

What flowers are under your nose?
Two-lips! LOL!

Where do sheep get their hair cut?
At the BAA-BAA shop! :)

What is a school bandleader's favorite date?

March 4th!

When do shoes get longer?
When two feet are added to them!

What's round on both sides and high in the middle?
O-HI-o! LOL!

Why did the sprinter go to the barber?

To shave off a few seconds of their time!

What's the difference between the North Pole and the South Pole?

All the difference in the world! HA HA HA!

What moves fastest, heat or cold?

Heat. You can catch cold!

What do basketball players and babies have in common?

They both dribble!

What does your uncle's wife put on her pizza?

AUNT-chovies! LOL!

How did the caboose learn to ride a bike?

With TRAIN-ing wheels!

What's a T-shirt's favorite game?

Tag! LOL!

Bill: What's a musician's favorite sandwich?
Jill: TUNE-a fish!

What has lots of teeth, but doesn't eat?

A comb!

What do aardvarks have that no other animal has?

Baby aardvarks!

Why do hummingbirds hum?

Because they can't remember the words! ROTFL!

Q: What does a seat belt do under pressure?
A: It buckles!

What kind of fish are found in the night sky?

Star fish!

What question can you never answer "yes" to?

"Are you sleeping?" LOL!

Which running shoe won the race?

Neither. They were tied! HEE-HEE!

What did the money wear to the wedding?

A BUCKS-edo!

Chapter 4

Tee-Hee!

What do cattle put on their salads?
Ranch dressing!

Ned: What is the second to last letter of the alphabet?

Zed: Y!

Ned: Because I want to know!

Why does no one believe the king of beasts?

He's always LION! GUFFAW!

What did the beaver say to the tree?

"It was nice getting to GNAW you!" ROTFL!

How does a frog greet another frog?

"WART"s up?!"

What do Henry the VIII and Kermit the Frog have in common?

They both have the same middle name!

46

How did the dog find a penny?

She followed the s-CENT! :D

How did the phone fly?

It was in airplane mode! HA HA HA!

Fred: How did the chef make spaghetti?
Jed: She used her noodle!

Why did the computer call in sick?

It had a virus! :)

What kind of ears does a train have?

Engin-EARS!

What time do you go to the dentist?
Tooth-Hurty! (2:30)

Moe: Why did the peach lose the car race?

Joe: It made too many PIT stops!

What do emails wear to see better?
Contacts!

What did the math teacher climb on vacation?

A SUM-mit!

What did zero say to eight?

"I like your belt!" LOL!

What do you order at a Ninja restaurant?

Kung FOOD!

Chapter 5

Jesting Fun!

Dad: What gets wet while it's drying?

Lad: A towel! LOL!

What do you call a kitten without an eye?

Ktten! ;)

What do you get when you cross a bee with an eagle?

A BEAGLE!

Why didn't the girl with no umbrella get wet?
It wasn't raining!

What's the best name for a school coach?

Jim!

What's the best name for an art teacher?

Artie! HEE-HEE!

Moe: Why did the gum cross the road?

Joe: It was stuck to a shoe!

Why did the house painter fall off the ladder?

They didn't know right from RUNG!

What frozen treat can you ride?

A pop-CYCLE! :)

How did the needle win the argument?

It had a good point! GUFFAW!

Why was the bunny frowning?

It was having a bad HARE day!

What is the longest word?

Smiles. There's a mile between each "s"! LOL!

What did the cartoonist's bumper sticker say?

"How am I DRAWING?"

What time is it if you meet an angry dog?

Time to run! ;)

What do you call an ostrich that is out of money?
Ost-POOR!

What did the dog say when he went on a cruise ship?

"BONE voyage!" HEE-HEE!

When is your hair like firecrackers?

When it has BANGS!

What animal do all the others look up to?

A giraffe! HEE-HEE!

Where did the boat go when it was sick?

To the DOCK-tor! LOL!

Why couldn't the girl finish her doughnut?

She couldn't eat the HOLE thing!

When do cats have eight legs?

When there are two of them!

What did the planet press on the keyboard?

The SPACE bar!

Chapter 6

Map Zap Part One

Which state disappeared?

Ore-GONE!

Mom: Which state do sheep like?
Tom: EWE-tah!

Which state does a crayon like?

COLOR-ado!

Which state is the smallest?

MINI-sota!

Which state has the most barbers?

New Hamp-SHEAR!

Which state goes to the doctor?
ILL-inois! HEE-HEE!

Which state is the friendliest?

O-HI-o!

Which state is a horse's favorite?
MANE!

Which state sees the best?

EYE-daho!

Which state shouts the loudest?

YELL-oware! ;)

Which state makes the most noise?

Ala-BAM-a!

Which state has the most weddings?

MARRY-land!

Which state uses the most scissors?

Connecti-CUT! :)

Which state do you walk on?
FLOOR-ida!

Which state takes the most baths?

WASH-ington!

Which state are baseball uniforms made in?

New JERSEY!

Which state is always asking questions?

WHY-oming! ROTFL!

Which state has the most trains?

Massa-CHOO-CHOO-setts!

Which is the best state to live in?
Okla-HOME-a!

Which state do your relatives live in?

Wis-COUSIN!

Which state raises the most pigs?

New PORK! HA HA HA!

Which state does a shirt live in?

Ken-TUCK-y!

Which state did the family go canoeing to?

ROWED Island!

Which state likes to take naps?
REST Virginia!

Which state are pencils made in?

PENCIL-vania! :D

Hawaii?
I'm fine. How are you?!

What's the capital of Texas?

T!

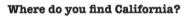

Where do you find California?

On a map!

Ned: What did Tennessee?

Ted: The same that Arkansas!

Which state has the most dogs?

COLLIE-fornia!

Which state has a stomachache?

MOAN-tana!

Which state has the most positive attitude?

Ar-CAN-sas!

Which state just went to the dentist?

Georgi-AHHH!

Which state has the funniest riddle?

Idaho...

I don't know either!

> **Moe:** Do you remember I lent you five dollars?
> **Joe:** Yeah, IOWA! (I owe ya!)

Which state is the least hard to live in?

Lou-EASY-ana!

Which state doesn't know what to say?

In...d'...and...uh! (Indiana!)

These state jokes are now officially over.

AT LAST-ka!

Map Zap Part Two

Less Is More!

Which state do pirates live in?

AR :)

Which state gives the most smooches?

KS

Which state has the most doctors?

MD

Which state needs to fill up the gas tank?

MT (HEE-HEE!)

Which state is your mom from?

MA

Which state is your dad from?

PA

Which state is always all right?

OK

Which state has a lot of waves?

HI

Which state is the most self-centered?

ME

LOL.

Which state is the most jealous?

NV :D (envy!)

Uncle Sam: AK! GA! ME, IA don't want NE MO!

Lady Liberty: OH! UT? OK! ND!

This Is Ridiculous!

What do you call a giraffe at the North Pole?

Lost!

What side of a cat has the most fur?

The outside! :D

Q: What do sheep wear in their wool?

A: Baaa-rettes! LOL!

What do you get when you cross a skunk with an elephant?

A SMELLY-phant!

What's red and makes a lot of noise?

A cardinal with a pair of cymbals!

Moe: What's black and white and black and white and black and white?

Joe: A skunk rolling down a mountain!

What do you call an orange parrot?

A carrot!

Q: What kind of dog likes to bake cookies?

A: Oven mutt! ROTFL!

What has spots and goes round and round?

A leopard on a Ferris wheel!

Why are bananas yellow?
So you can tell them apart from elephants!

First pig: Oink!

Second pig: Meow!

First pig: Why'd you say that?!

Second pig: I'm learning a foreign language!

Why do birds fly south?

It's faster than walking! ;)

What should a ship avoid at school?

PIER pressure! :D

What do you call bears with no ears?

B! GUFFAW!

Old MacDonald Had a Joke...

What do you get when you cross guacamole with a bird?

SQUACK-amole! LOL!

What do you get when you cross guacamole with a rollercoaster?

Guaca-HOLY-MOLEY!!!

When the frog ordered a hamburger, what did the waiter say?

"Do you want FLIES with that?"

What animal shouldn't you play a game with?

A CHEETAH!

Gracie: What kind of dog can tell time?

Stacey: A WATCH dog!

Cowboy: What looks like half a horse?

Cowgirl: The other half!

Why aren't Dalmatians good at playing hide-and-seek?

Because they're always spotted! CHORTLE!

How do bees cross town?

On a crosstown BUZZ!

What do you say to a frog on its birthday?

"HOPPY birthday!"

What do you say to a sad lightbulb?

"Brighten up!"

What do you call a horsefly when it goes away?

A horse-FLEW! HA HA HA!

What has four legs and two tails?

A cat flipping a coin! HA HA HA!

Why didn't the lemon win the race?

It ran out of juice!

What kind of sandwiches do you find in the ocean?

Peanut butter and JELLYFISH sandwich!

What did the goose say when he got scared?
"Look at my people bumps!" CHORTLE!

Is This Your Idea of a Joke?

How can butterflies fly?

They WING it!

What did one statue say to the other statue?

"Don't take me for GRANITE!" LOL!

What did the toaster say to the clock?

"Got a minute?"

Q: Which bird is a bully?
A: A MOCKING-bird! :)

Q: Where do fish keep their money?

A: A river bank!

Q: Where do penguins keeps their money?
A: In a snow bank!

What do you get if you cross a parrot with a shark?

A bird that talks your ear off! :D

What did the glue say to the paper?

"Stick with me!" ROTFL!

What do you call a duck that tells riddles?

A wise-QUACKER!

What do you call a bull taking a nap?

A bull-DOZER! HA HA HA!

What planet has the most music?
Nep-TUNE!

What is one of the most beautiful landmarks in the world?

The EYE-FULL Tower!

What is yellow and black and white?

A school bus full of Dalmatians! ;)

Why did the kid take a baseball bat and a grocery bag to bed?

It was time to hit the sack!

On what day does a robin wear shorts?

Casual FLY-day! ROTFL!

What has two humps and is found in Cleveland?

A lost camel!

What did the veggie burger say to the cow?
Nothing! Veggie burgers can't talk!

What's the best time to buy a chicken?

When it's going CHEEP!

Q: What did the plate say about the sandwich?
A: "Lunch is on me!"

What has four wheels and flies?

A garbage truck!

Chapter 7

FUNZieS

Floral Funnies

Which flowers are the most grateful?

A GLAD-ioli! GUFFAW!

Which flowers like kisses?
Tu-LIPS!

Which flower is the silliest?

A DAFFY-dil!

Which flower is good on toast?

BUTTER-cup!

Which flower can you find at the zoo?

A dande-LION!

Which flower can you drive to the zoo?
A CAR-nation!

Which flower is very quiet?

Chrysanthe-MUM!

Which flower is a frog's favorite?
A CROAK-us!

With which flower can you row a boat?

An OAR-chid!

With which flower do you fry an egg?
A PAN-sy!

Which flower is like a dog or cat?

A PET-unia!

Which flower is always proper?
A PRIM-rose!

Chapter 8

Yuk-Yuks!

What part of Cleveland is in Delaware?

The letter D!

What do you call a pig that knows karate?

Pork chops! :)

Ned: How do turtles call each other?

Ted: On their SHELL phones! HA HA HA!

Why do you go to the barber shop when it's hot?

They have HAIR-conditioning!

What goes "krab, krab!"?

A dog barking backwards!

What goes "woem, woem!"?

Aww, come on, you can guess that one!

What do you call a scarecrow that plays outfield?
Outstanding in their field! :D

Q: What do owls say when they cry?

A: Boo-WHO!

Bromilla: What does a watch say when it's hungry?

Camilla: "May I please have seconds?" HEE-HEE!

What do you tell a mattress when it gets on an airplane?
"Fasten your SHEET belt!"

When is a car not a car?

When it turns into a garage!

What kind of ant is good at math?
An account-ANT! GUFFAW!

Dad Jokes!

Gym teacher: Can you stand on your head?

Silly Billy: No, I can't step up that high!

Why did the beach cross the road?
To get to the other TIDE!

What kind of book does a stink bug write?

Best SMELLERS! ;)

Q: What do you call a goldfish that met a piranha?

A: Dinner!

Q: What do elephants wear to the swimming pool?

A: Swimming trunks!

Why did the box of pencils win the game?

It had the most points!

Why did the chicken tell riddles to her egg?

She wanted it to crack up! :D

Brock: Thanks, Doctor, for treating my hoarse throat!
Doc: Sure! Here's my bill, PONY UP!

What do you do if you find an elephant in your bathtub?

You pull the plug! ROTFL!

What did the stove say to the pan?

"Pleased to HEAT you!"

What did the sheep say to the dog?

"Please to BLEAT you!"

What did the hamburger say to the bun?

"Pleased to MEAT you!"

What did the chair say to the cushion?

"Pleased to SEAT you!"

Silly Millie: How does a wet dog smell?
Silly Billie: Through its nose!

When John, Paul, George, and Ringo went on stage, who was the fifth Beatle?

Mike! :)

Why did the banana call in sick?

It wasn't PEELING good!

What do you call a boomerang that doesn't come back?

A stick! HA HA HA!

What's a police officer's favorite dessert?

A COP-cake!

Ned: What did you get for your birthday?

Ted: Older!

What do dogs do when they want a chuckle?

Chew on a FUNNYBONE! LOL!

What dog won't bark when you bite it?

A HOT DOG!

Chapter 9

School Nurse Jokes!
Part One

> **Abner:** My nose is running!
> **Nurse Nancy:** You'd better catch it!

Nurse Nancy: Have your eyes ever been checked?

Aiden: No, they've always been brown!

Sophia: I'm sick like a dog!

Nurse: You better go to the vet!

Jackson: I swallowed a recorder in music class!

Nurse Nancy: It's a good thing you weren't playing the drums!

Olivia: I accidentally swallowed my lunch money!

Nurse Nancy: I'll pat you on the back, and you'll see some change!

Ethan: I accidentally swallowed a sheep!

Nurse Nancy: Do you feel baaaaa-d?

Isabella: My leg hurts when I do this!

Nurse Nancy: Then don't do it!

Liam: Sometimes I feel like I'm a goat!

Nurse Nancy: How long's this been going on?

Liam: Since I was a little kid!

Emilia: I can't remember anything!

Nurse Nancy: When did this start?

Emilia: When did what start?

John: I think I'm an electric drill!

Nurse Nancy: That must be very boring!

Kyli: I think I'm a yo-yo!

Nurse Nancy: Are you having ups and downs?

Theresa: There's a fly buzzing around my head!

Nurse Nancy: Don't worry, it's just a bug going around!

Giuliano: I think I'm a cell phone!

Nurse Nancy: If you're not better tomorrow, give me a ring!

Giuliana: I think I'm a pencil!

Nurse Nancy: I see your point!

Matthew: I think I'm a dog!

Nurse Nancy: Sit on the chair, and let's talk about this!

Matthew: But I'm not allowed to sit on the furniture!

Matt: I have something stuck in my throat!

Nurse Nancy: Are you choking?!

Matt: No, I'm serious!

Gabriella: I see spots in front of my eyes!

Nurse Nancy: Have you seen an eye doctor?

Gabriella: No, just spots!

Gabby: I think I'm a bridge!

Nurse Nancy: What's come over you?

Gabby: Six cars and an ice cream truck!

Kyle: I'm seeing double!

Nurse Nancy: Sit down on the chair please!

Kyle: Which one?!

Ha Ha Ha Ha Ha!

Why shouldn't you tell secrets on a farm?

Because the corn has ears, the potatoes have eyes, and the beanstalk! (beans talk ;))

Mat: What's the best thing to put in a pie?

Pat: Your teeth!

What's the hardest thing about learning to ride a skateboard?

The sidewalk!

Why is camping so exciting?

Because it is intense! (In tents! :))

Why is tennis such a noisy game?

Because the players always raise a racket!

Why would a spider be a good outfielder?

Because it's good at catching flies! LOL!

Art teacher: What color should you make the wind and the sun?

Kid: The wind blue and the sun rose!

Why couldn't the bear go into the store?

It had bear feet! (No shoes, no service!)

Zoe: What can jump higher than a big rock?
Zack: Anything! Rocks can't jump!

What game does a plumber like to play?

Hide-and-LEAK! CHORTLE!

What game does a gentle person like to play?

Hide-and-MEEK! :D

What game does a computer programmer like to play?

Hide-and-GEEK!

What game does a skunk like to play?
Hide-and-REEK! LOL!

Where can you always find help?

In the dictionary! :)

Where is a pony born?

In the HORSE-pital!

Lifeguard: If you fell into the water, what's the first thing you'd do?

Swimmer: Get wet!

When do frogs get married?

On a LEAP year! LOL!

What has a tail, six legs, and two heads?

A boy riding a horse! ;)

What does a farmer grow, if they work super hard?

Tired!

Why did the cafeteria lady put the chicken in the school garden?

She was trying to grow an EGG-plant! LOL!

Silly Questions & Answers:

How long have you had that birthmark?

Since I was born!

Where do you find kangaroos?

Wherever you left them!

Why did the science teacher bring the turtle to school?

It needed to come out of its shell!

What did the silly dog do?

Chase parked cars!

What never get cold in a refrigerator?

Hot sauce!

Alphabetical Antics!

What starts with T, ends with T, and is full of T?

A teapot! CHORTLE!

Why is the letter A like a flower?

Because a B is always after it!

How is the letter A and noon alike?

They're both in the middle of day!

What three letters are the opposite of a friend?

N-M-E! (Enemy ;))

What letter is always having a good time?

The letter U, because it's always in the middle of FUN!

What two letters aren't good for your teeth?

DK (Decay! ;))

What two letters mean it's cold weather?

I-C (Icy) ;)

Goofy Gags!

Lad: Why do I have to go to bed every night?

Dad: Because your bed won't come to you! :)

Why did the rhinoceros ring the bell on his tricycle?

Because his horn wasn't working!

Moe: What tree is as small as your hand?

Joe: A palm tree! :D

Action figure: Do you wanna go get something to eat?

Teddy bear: No thanks, I'm stuffed! HA HA HA!

The Biggers just had a baby. Now who is bigger?
The baby. He is a little Bigger!

> **What's worse than raining cats and dogs?**
> HAILING taxis!

What musical instrument do you find by the sink?

A TUBA toothpaste! HEE-HEE!

What kind of food do polar bears like?

Cold slaw! :P

School Nurse Jokes!
Part Two

Katlin: Can I have a second opinion?

Nurse Nancy: Sure, come back after lunch!

Matthew: I think I'm coming down with something!

Nurse Nancy: Maybe you're an elevator!

Heather: I'm so very tired!

Nurse Nancy: Run around your bed at night to catch up on your sleep!

Nurse Nancy: Why do you want me to examine your math book?

Alexa: Because it has a lot of problems!

Ava: I have a potato growing out of my nose!

Nurse Nancy: How did that happen?

Ava: I don't know. I planted carrots!

Mason: I'm worried because I accidentally swallowed my pencil!

Nurse Nancy: Ok, write down these instructions...

Lily: Do you think I have poison ivy?

Nurse Nancy: I don't want to make a rash judgment!

Griffin: I'm shrinking!

Nurse Nancy: I'll see you in a moment—be a little patient!

Grace: Whenever I drink hot chocolate, I get a pain in my eye!

Nurse Nancy: Take the spoon out of the mug first!

Elina: I think I'm a caterpillar!

Nurse Nancy: Don't fret. You'll soon see a change!

Robin: I can't catch the ball in gym class!

Nurse Nancy: Don't worry. It's not catching!

Brenda: I think I'm a frog!

Nurse Nancy: You'll be ok!

Brenda: But I feel like I'm gonna croak!

Chapter 10

DID YOU hear THIS ONE?!

So Funny!

Which is the shortest month?

May, it only has three letters!

Math teacher: If I had three baseballs in one hand and five baseballs in the other, what would I have?

Griffin: WOW! Very big hands! :P

Math teacher: How many sides does a crayon box have?

Grace: Two, the inside and the outside!

Mr. Beecher the Teacher: What goes all around the playground, but never moves?

Sid the Kid: The fence!

Teacher: Name five animals from the North Pole!

Silly Billy: Two seals and three polar bears!

What smells most when you encounter a skunk?
Your nose! ;)

What's the best day to work on your tan?

SUN-day!

Frog + dog = Croaker Spaniel!

Gorilla + porcupine = 350 pound hairbrush!

Cereal + snow = Corn flakes!

Snowball + shark = Frost bite!

Superhero Jokes!

Where does Clark Kent play football?

In the SUPER bowl!

What do you call a supervillain that's kind and caring?

A total failure!

What do you call superheroes that eat omelettes for breakfast?

The EGGS-men!

Which superhero wears the biggest boots?

The one with the biggest feet!

Where do you find Spider-Man on the computer?
On his website!

How do you talk to Ant-Man?

Use little words!

What do you call Ant-Man when he gets old?

An Ant-ique!

Why doesn't Ant-Man get sick?
He's full of ant-ibodies!

Why is Superman never afraid?

He has nerves of steel!

What size costume does Superman wear?

Size S! :)

Griffin: What's green and flies?

Grace: Super Pickle!

Why was The Flash in such a hurry?

He had the runs!

What do you get when you cross Barry Allen with Peter Parker?

Speeder-Man! ;P

Chapter 11

CHAPTERS OF CHUCKLES!

LOL!

Nutty Jokes!

What kind of nut is part of a room?

A WALL-nut!

What nut is found along the ocean?

A BEACH-nut!

What nut sounds like a sneeze?

A cashew nut!

What nut has a hole in it?

A DOUGH-nut!

Riddle Me This

What goes through a door but never goes in or out?

A keyhole!

What's at the end of a rainbow?

The letter W!

Michael: If an orange house is made of orange bricks and a brown house is made of brown bricks, what is a greenhouse made of?

Rachael: Glass!

If two's company and three's a crowd, what are four and five?

Nine!

What word can you add a syllable to and it becomes shorter?

Short! :D

What wears shoes but has no feet?

A sidewalk!

What begins with P, ends with E, and has over a hundred letters in it?

A post office!

How many books can you carry in an empty backpack?

None! The backpack's empty! LOL!

What kind of water can't freeze?

Boiling water!

What goes up, but never goes down?

Your age! :P

About the Author

Vice magazine has called Yoe the "Indiana Jones of comics historians." *Publisher Weekly* says he's the "archivist of the ridiculous and the sublime" and calls his work "brilliant." *The Onion* calls him a "celebrated designer," *The Library Journal* says, "a comics guru." BoingBoing hails him "a fine cartoonist and a comic book historian of the first water." Yoe was creative director/vice president/general manager of Jim Henson's Muppets, and a creative director at Nickelodeon and Disney. Craig has won multiple Eisner Awards and the Gold Medal from the Society of Illustrators.

Mango Publishing, established in 2014, publishes an eclectic list of books by diverse authors—both new and established voices—on topics ranging from business, personal growth, women's empowerment, LGBTQ studies, health, and spirituality to history, popular culture, time management, decluttering, lifestyle, mental wellness, aging, and sustainable living. We were recently named 2019's #1 fastest growing independent publisher by Publishers Weekly. Our success is driven by our main goal, which is to publish high quality books that will entertain readers as well as make a positive difference in their lives.

Our readers are our most important resource; we value your input, suggestions, and ideas. We'd love to hear from you—after all, we are publishing books for you!

Please stay in touch with us and follow us at:

Facebook: Mango Publishing

Twitter: @MangoPublishing

Instagram: @MangoPublishing

LinkedIn: Mango Publishing

Pinterest: Mango Publishing

Sign up for our newsletter at www.mangopublishinggroup.com and receive a free book!

Join us on Mango's journey to reinvent publishing, one book at a time.

9 781642 502381